BIGELOW FREE PUBLIC LIBRARY
54 WALNUT STREET
CLINTON, MA 01510

BIGELOW FREE PUBLIC LIBRARY
54 WALNUT STREET
CLINTON, MA 01510

BIGELOW FREE PUBLIC LIBRARY
11/5/09
#197.365
CLINTON, MASS.

HEAD-TO-TOE HEALTH

FOOD ALLERGIES

ELAINE LANDAU

Marshall Cavendish
Benchmark
New York

Marshall Cavendish Benchmark
99 White Plains Road
Tarrytown, New York 10591
www.marshallcavendish.us

Expert Reader: Leslie L. Barton, MD, Professor Emerita of Pediatrics,
University of Arizona College of Medicine, Tucson, Arizona

© 2010 Elaine Landau

All rights reserved.

No part of this book may be reproduced in any form without the written permission of the copyright holders.
All Internet addresses were correct and accurate at the time of printing.

Library of Congress Cataloging-in-Publication Data

Landau, Elaine.
Food allergies / by Elaine Landau.
p. cm. — (Head-to-toe health)
Includes bibliographical references and index.
Summary: "Provides basic information about food allergies and their prevention"—Provided by publisher.
  ISBN 978-0-7614-3500-6
  1. Food allergy—Juvenile literature. I. Title.
  RC596.L36 2010
  616.97'5—dc22   2008010785

Editor: Christine Florie
Publisher: Michelle Bisson
Art Director: Anahid Hamparian
Series Designer: Alex Ferrari

Photo research by Candlepants Incorporated

Cover Photo: Steven Mark Needham/Envision/Corbis

The photographs in this book are used by permission and through the courtesy of:
Alamy Images: Superstock, 4; Bubbles Photolibrary, 13; Steven May, 22. *Photo Researchers Inc.*: Ken Cavanagh, 7; John Bavosi, 11; Mark Thomas, 23. *Corbis*: Envision, 15; Paul Barton, 17; Erik Freeland, 25. *Getty Images*: SIU/Visuals Unlimited, 20.

Printed in Malaysia
1 3 5 6 4 2

Contents

IT WAS JUST A BITE . . . 5

HAVING A FOOD ALLERGY . . . 9

THE SCOOP ON FOOD ALLERGIES . . . 14

IS IT A FOOD ALLERGY? . . . 18

STAYING SAFE AND WELL . . . 21

GLOSSARY . . . 27

FIND OUT MORE . . . 28

INDEX . . . 30

It Was Just a Bite

It started off as a great day. Your school was having a food fair. Everyone brought in a special dish from home.

There were lots of great things to eat. You just had to decide what to pick. You are **allergic** to nuts. It's dangerous for you to eat nuts or anything made with them.

That meant that you'd have to pass on the banana nut cake and the fudge and walnut brownies. That didn't matter, though. You already knew what you really wanted.

It was a delicious-looking vanilla cupcake. The cupcake was topped with fluffy strawberry icing—your favorite. Yet you didn't bite into the cupcake right away. A scary thought crossed your mind. Were there tiny nut bits on top of the frosting?

You asked the kid who brought in the cupcakes. He didn't know. Now it was up to you to decide what to do. You wondered if it was okay to take a chance—just this once.

◀ **If you've eaten something that you're allergic to, it takes only minutes for symptoms to begin.**

You were sure that you would be fine. Besides, you're always so careful. You felt that you deserved a treat.

So you bit into the cupcake. You ate the icing first because that's the best part. Sadly, you never got a chance to get to the cake part.

Within minutes, your face swelled up. Your skin itched. There was a tingling feeling in your mouth. Your throat tightened, too. Soon you found it hard to breathe.

Your teacher rushed to your aid. By then, you knew you had made the wrong choice.

Even a few nut bits can make you very ill. No food is worth doing that to yourself. Nothing tastes that good—not even a cupcake with fluffy strawberry icing.

THAT FOOD IS A NO-NO!

The student described here has a food allergy. That young person is not alone. It's thought that about 2 million children—nearly 8 percent of children in the United States—have food allergies. About 4 percent of adults in the United States have them as well.

Most people enjoy eating. That's true of people who have food allergies, too. Yet they must be careful. Eating the wrong food can be harmful to them.

Food allergies affect different people in different ways. For some, a food allergy may just cause hives. Others might get a bad stomachache.

For still others, food allergies are more serious. They can become very ill. If they don't get help right away, some may even die.

Nevertheless, most people with food allergies lead full and happy lives. They enjoy most foods. They learn to avoid

Some food allergies can give people a stomachache.

foods that can hurt them. They also learn what to do if they eat the wrong thing.

This book is all about food allergies. By the time you finish it, you'll know everything you need to know about them. Unlike the foods you may be allergic to, nothing in this book is harmful. So dig in and keep reading. You'll find lots of helpful and interesting facts here.

TASTY TROUBLEMAKERS

Do you know which foods cause most food allergies in young children? They are milk, eggs, peanuts, and tree nuts. A tree nut is a nut that grows on a tree, such as a walnut, pecan, or cashew. Besides nuts, fish and shellfish are the foods that most often cause allergic reactions in older children and teens.

Having a Food Allergy

Oh, no! It's happening again. You ate shrimp and you feel sick. First, you were nauseous. Your stomach hurt, too. It wasn't long before you threw up. You felt a little better for a few minutes. But then you had to get to the bathroom—really fast. It was **diarrhea**!

This can happen if you eat a food you are allergic to. There can be other **symptoms** as well. Some people with food allergies become only mildly sick. Others become very ill very quickly.

However, still others eat the same foods that make people with food allergies sick and nothing happens to them. So just what happens to someone who has a food allergy?

YOUR IMMUNE SYSTEM GOOFS

It all has to do with the body's **immune system**. Your immune system is important. It protects you from germs that can hurt you.

Yet when you have a food allergy, your immune system makes a terrible mistake. It happens every time you eat that particular food. Your immune system acts as if a harmless food is really dangerous to you.

It starts to do this by making **antibodies**. Antibodies act as the body's soldiers. They spring into action to protect you from harmful germs.

The immune system creates antibodies to the food you are allergic to. These antibodies, in turn, attach themselves to a type of immune system cell known as a mast cell.

THE TROUBLE BEGINS

When you eat a food you are allergic to, things are set in motion. The mast cells release a lot of chemicals. One of these chemicals, called **histamine**, is especially troublesome. Histamine causes the symptoms experienced by people with allergies.

People may feel itchy, break out in hives, or get stomach cramps. Some vomit and have diarrhea. There may also be tightness in the throat and swelling of the lips and tongue, as well as trouble with breathing.

This illustration shows mast cells during an allergic reaction. Histamine (tiny red balls above) is released, causing allergic symptoms.

PEOPLE REACT DIFFERENTLY

Some people with food allergies only get one or two symptoms. Others get more. Often people react quickly—most allergic reactions occur within an hour. Some get sick within minutes of eating the food, while for others it may take up to two hours.

The worst cases of food allergies result in **anaphylaxis**. This is a serious condition that affects many parts of the body, including the heart, lungs, and kidneys, among others.

HOW MUCH IS TOO MUCH?

Question: Do you have to have a large helping of the food you're allergic to before you get sick?
Answer: No. Some people with food allergies can get sick just by touching the food or breathing it in! What if someone with a peanut allergy kisses someone who has just had a peanut butter and jelly sandwich? The person with the peanut allergy can get sick. This can happen even if the person who ate the sandwich brushed his or her teeth.

When anaphylaxis occurs, the person may have trouble breathing. There can also be a drop in blood pressure. The heart rate slows and the kidneys may also shut down.

Someone suffering from this condition can soon lose consciousness and even die. The risk is very real. Therefore, it's important that the person get help right away. Severe food allergies result in about 30,000 emergency room visits each year.

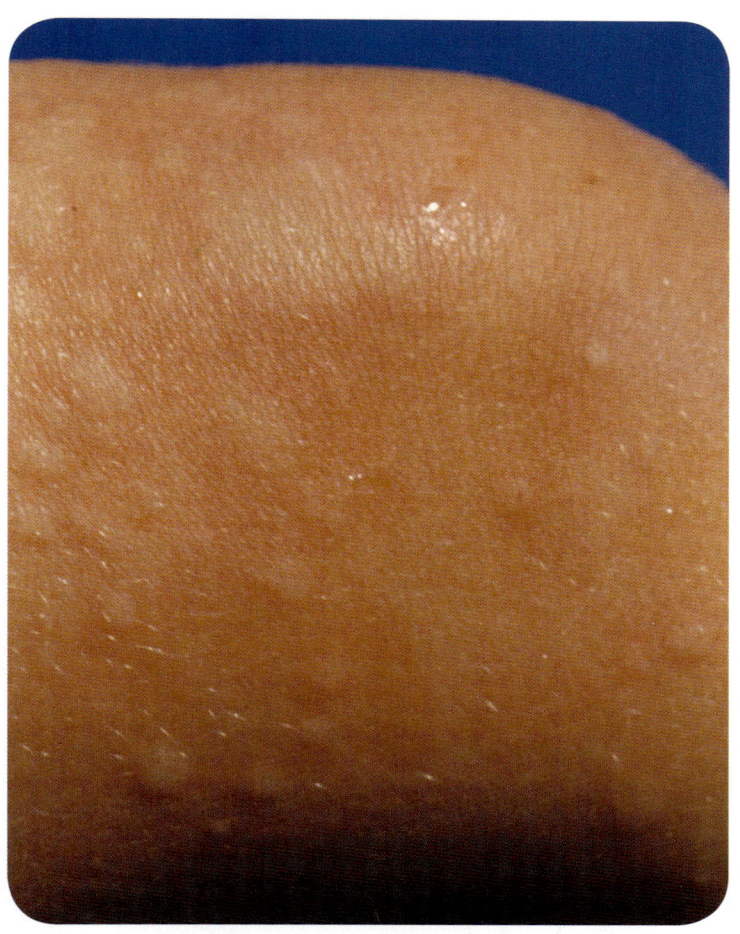

This person broke out in hives after eating a plum. Hives are a symptom of a food allergy.

The Scoop on Food Allergies

DID YOU KNOW?

Where you live has something to do with the foods you're allergic to. In Japan, people eat lots of rice. Guess what? Rice allergies are common there. In Scandinavia, fish is often served. Many Scandinavians are allergic to codfish.

How much do you know about food allergies? The more you know, the safer you'll be. So it's important to learn as much as you can about them. Try answering this true or false question: Once you have a food allergy you'll always have it. False. Young people sometimes outgrow their allergies. However, you are more likely to outgrow allergies to eggs, milk, or soy rather than to peanuts.

WHY DO SOME PEOPLE GET FOOD ALLERGIES?

Have you ever wondered why some people get food allergies? That's not an easy question to answer. Even scientists are not sure of the answer.

Some think that allergies may be tied to being very clean. That sounds strange, but it makes sense. Just think about it for a minute.

The United States has clean water. Liquid and solid waste is quickly carried away through drains and sewers. **Vaccines** keep people safe from many diseases.

People don't come in contact with a lot of dangerous germs that are common elsewhere, so their bodies don't develop a resistance to them. Instead, their bodies may

This is a grouping of the most common foods that people are allergic to.

begin to battle more harmless things; in some cases, these may be foods like eggs or wheat.

Others think that allergies are linked to how soon young children eat different foods. What if peanuts are given to very young children? Are they more likely to become allergic to them?

Some scientists say yes! They point to what happened in England and Australia. Parents there began giving their very young children peanut butter and jelly sandwiches. Sure enough, the number of kids with peanut allergies shot up.

A third thought about allergies has to do with family history. Food allergies often run in families. Let's say that one or both parents in a family have a food allergy. Their children are more likely to have the allergy, too.

Which of these ideas is right? Maybe there is more than one answer. Perhaps all these things play a part in why people get allergies.

Yet one thing is certain. Food allergies are on the rise in the United States. Scientists hope to learn more about their causes. That way, they can better help people with food allergies. They might even find ways to avoid getting allergies in the first place!

Some food allergies are passed on from parents to their children.

Is It A Food Allergy?

Think you may have a food allergy? Do you break out in a rash or hives when you eat a certain food? Perhaps you vomit or have cramps whenever you have that food.

If this happens to you, you may need to see an **allergist**. When you go to an allergist, get ready for lots of questions.

The doctor will want to know:

1. How much of the food you ate when you got sick.
2. How long it took before you felt sick.
3. If you always feel sick when you eat this food.

Your answers will help the doctor decide if you have a food allergy. The doctor may also do some allergy tests. This helps the doctor find exactly what food or foods are causing the problem.

OH, NO! THAT FOOD'S GOTTA GO!

Has a food allergy landed you in the doctor's office? Do you think you know which food is causing the problem? The doctor may ask you to stay away from that food for a while. After you take the food away, does the problem go away, too? If so, then you are probably allergic to that food. This test is called an elimination diet.

TESTING, TESTING, TESTING

One test is known as a skin prick test. Here, the doctor puts a drop of a specific food on your arm or back. The food is in liquid form, so it won't look like the food you eat.

Then the doctor scratches your skin with a needle. A tiny amount of the liquid goes into your skin.

Will your body react? If so, there'll be redness or swelling at the spot in about fifteen minutes, which means you are probably allergic to the food tested.

There are other allergy tests, too. Some doctors use blood tests. With these tests, a sample of your blood is sent to a medical laboratory.

At the lab, the blood is tested. The test shows if there are any antibodies to certain foods. This helps your doctor know if you're allergic to those foods.

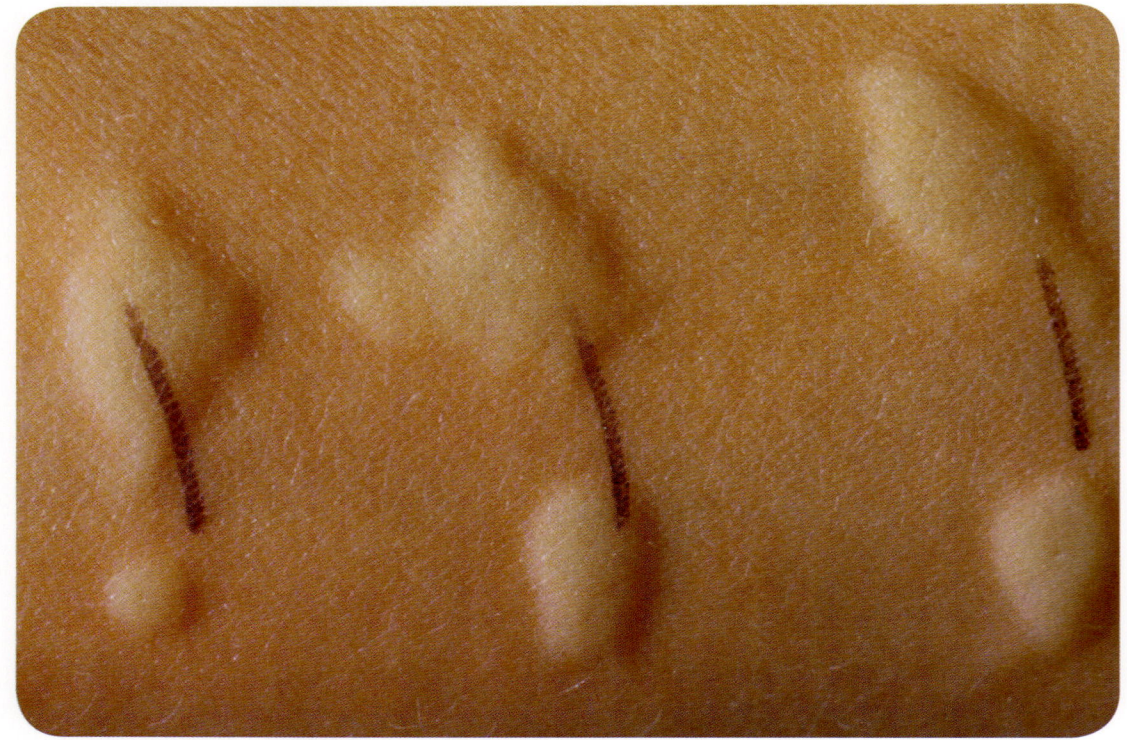

After a skin prick test, this person's skin became swollen. The raised bumps indicate an allergic reaction.

Staying Safe and Well

**Go away, stay away.
I can't eat you.
You're not okay!**

What if you could talk to food? You might say this to a food you're allergic to. Of course, you don't talk to food—you eat it. But you can say this to yourself when offered foods you shouldn't eat.

Right now, there's no cure for food allergies. You can't take a pill to make them disappear. That doesn't mean you have to take chances, though.

Just be sure to stay away from foods you can't eat. Become an expert label reader. Whatever is in a food must

Reading food labels carefully is a must if you are allergic to certain foods.

be listed on the label. That's the law. That also helps protect you.

HAVE AN ACTION PLAN

It's important to choose your foods carefully. But sometimes, anyone can make a mistake. You may accidentally eat a food you're allergic to. If this should happen, be prepared.

Every person with an allergy needs an action plan. An action plan spells out what to do if you react to a food.

You doctor or another health care provider can help you make up your action plan.

Your parents and school need to know your plan well, too. So does anyone else who takes care of you. Yet the plan will be most important to you.

If you react to a food, don't be scared. Just remember your plan and put it into action. Part of your plan is knowing who to tell. You must also know what medicines you need right away.

This is vital if your allergy causes anaphylaxis. Then you may need a

This girl wears an EpiPen around her neck. It contains epinephrine which treats allergic reactions.

quick shot of a medicine called **epinephrine**. Some kids carry this drug with them or a teacher or school nurse keeps it for them.

After getting the epinephrine, you'll feel better. But don't go back to what you were doing. Instead, you should contact your doctor. You may need to go to a hospital or medical center. This is important to be sure that you're really all right.

LIVING WITH A FOOD ALLERGY

Having a food allergy is never fun. But that doesn't mean that your life can't be rich and wonderful. There are still many tasty foods for you to enjoy.

Use these to replace the foods you can't eat. You may have already had a dairy-free birthday cake. Perhaps you've been invited to a no-peanut Halloween party, too.

Schools are now more helpful as well. Many have allergy-free zones in their cafeterias. These are tables where kids with allergies can safely eat with their friends. The foods that cause allergies are not allowed at these tables.

You may outgrow some food allergies. Others you won't. However, you can handle your allergies by becoming your own action hero.

Even if you are allergic to some foods, with care, you can enjoy many wonderful things to eat.

Action is the key word here. Always remember to read labels carefully. Let's say you want to try a new candy bar. Don't buy it until you read what's inside it.

If you should react to a food, put your action plan to work. Learn what to do by heart. You may have to battle food allergies, but this is a fight you can win!

Glossary

allergic — having an unpleasant or dangerous bodily reaction to something

allergist — a doctor who treats people who are allergic (see above) to various things

anaphylaxis — a dangerous condition that can cause swelling to the tongue and throat as well as trouble breathing

antibodies — the body's fighters against infection and disease

diarrhea — a condition in which bodily waste materials become loose and runny. Bowel movements are also more frequent.

epinephrine — a medicine used to fight a severe reaction to a food

histamine — a chemical released by some of the body's cells during an allergic (see above) reaction

immune system — the bodily system that protects you against germs

symptoms — signs of an illness

vaccines — a medicine given to protect a person from disease or illness

Find Out More

BOOKS

Glaser, Jason. *Food Allergies*. Mankato, MN: Capstone Press, 2007.

Johnson, Rebecca. *The Digestive System*. Minneapolis, MN: Lerner, 2005.

Koster, Gloria. *The Peanut-Free Café*. New York: Albert Whitman, 2006.

Llewellyn, Claire. *Eating*. North Mankato, MN: Smart Apple Media, 2005.

Powell, Jillian. *Aneil Has a Food Allergy*. Langhorne, PA: Chelsea Clubhouse, 2004.

Wallace, Holly. *Cells and Systems*. Chicago: Heinemann Library, 2007.

DVD

Alexander the Elephant Goes to School. The Food Allergy & Anaphylaxis Network, 2007.

WEB SITES

The Food Allergy Web Site Just for Kids

www.fankids.org

This is a great Web site for lots of info on food allergies. Don't miss the activities link for some fun things to do.

Just for Kids—Allergies

www.aaaai.org/patients/just4kids

See this Web site for some great puzzles, school projects, and games on allergies.

Index

Page numbers in **boldface** are illustrations.

action plan, 22–24
adults with food allergies, 6
allergic, 5–6, 27
allergist, 18–20, 27
allergy-free zones, 24
anaphylaxis, 12–13, 27
antibodies, 10, 27

blood pressure, 13
blood test, 19–20
breathing difficulty, 6, 10, 13

causes of allergies, 15–16
children with food allergies, 6
common food allergies, 8, **15**

cramps, stomach, 7, 9, 10

diagnosing allergies, 18–20
diarrhea, 9, 10, 27

elimination diet, 19
emergency room visits, 13
epinephrine, **23**, 23–24, 27

family history, 16
food labels, 21–22, **22**, 26
frequency of food allergies, 6

genetics and family history, 16
geographic location, 14

germs, 10, 15

heart rate, 13
histamine, 10, **11**, 27
hives, 7, 10, 13

immune system, 10, 27

Japan, 14

kidney function, 13

labels, food, 21–22, **22**, 26
lip/tongue swelling, 10
living with allergies, 5–6, 6–8, 21–24, 26
location, geographic, 14

mast cells, 10, **11**
medical diagnosing/testing, 18–**20**, 20

outgrowing allergies, 14, 24

people with food allergies, 6

reaction time, 12
reasons for allergies, 15–16

safety, 21–24, 26
Scandinavia, 14
skin prick test, 19, **20**
stomachaches, 7, 9, 10
swelling, lips and tongue, 10
symptoms, allergy, 6, 7, 9, 10, 12–13, 27

tests for allergies, 19–20, **20**
treatment for allergies, 21–24

vaccines, 15, 27

About the Author

Award-winning author Elaine Landau has written more than three hundred books for young readers. Many of these are on health and science topics. For Marshall Cavendish, Landau has written *Asthma*; *Bites and Stings*; *Broken Bones*; *Bumps, Bruises, and Scrapes*; *Cavities and Toothaches*; and *The Common Cold* for the Head-to-Toe Health series.

Landau received a bachelor's degree in English and journalism from New York University and a master's degree in library and information science from Pratt Institute. You can visit Elaine Landau at her Web site: www.elainelandau.com.

BIGELOW FREE PUBLIC LIBRARY
54 WALNUT STREET
CLINTON, MA 01510

#197.365   57

BIGELOW FREE PUBLIC LIBRARY
54 WALNUT STREET
CLINTON, MA 01510

SOCAL LOWRIDERS

BAD HABITS
GOOD TIMES

DECEMBER 2024   VOLUME 22

VOLUME 22

FRANKS HATS

FEATURE PHOTOGRAPHERS

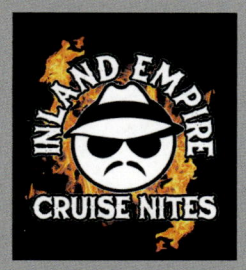

- SWAGGY SHOOTZ BY JUSTIN CODY
- UNIQUE PHOTOGRAPHY High Desert
- CALI CLASSICS CHINO CALIFORNIA
- INLAND EMPIRE CRUISE NITES

IT'S NOT JUST A HOBBY; IT'S A LIFESTYLE.

TAIL LIGHT TUESDAY

throw back

SWAGGY SHOOTZ

@SWAGGYSHOOTZ
BY JUSTIN CODY

throw back

**BAD HABITS
GOOD TIMES**

**BAD HABITS
GOOD TIMES**

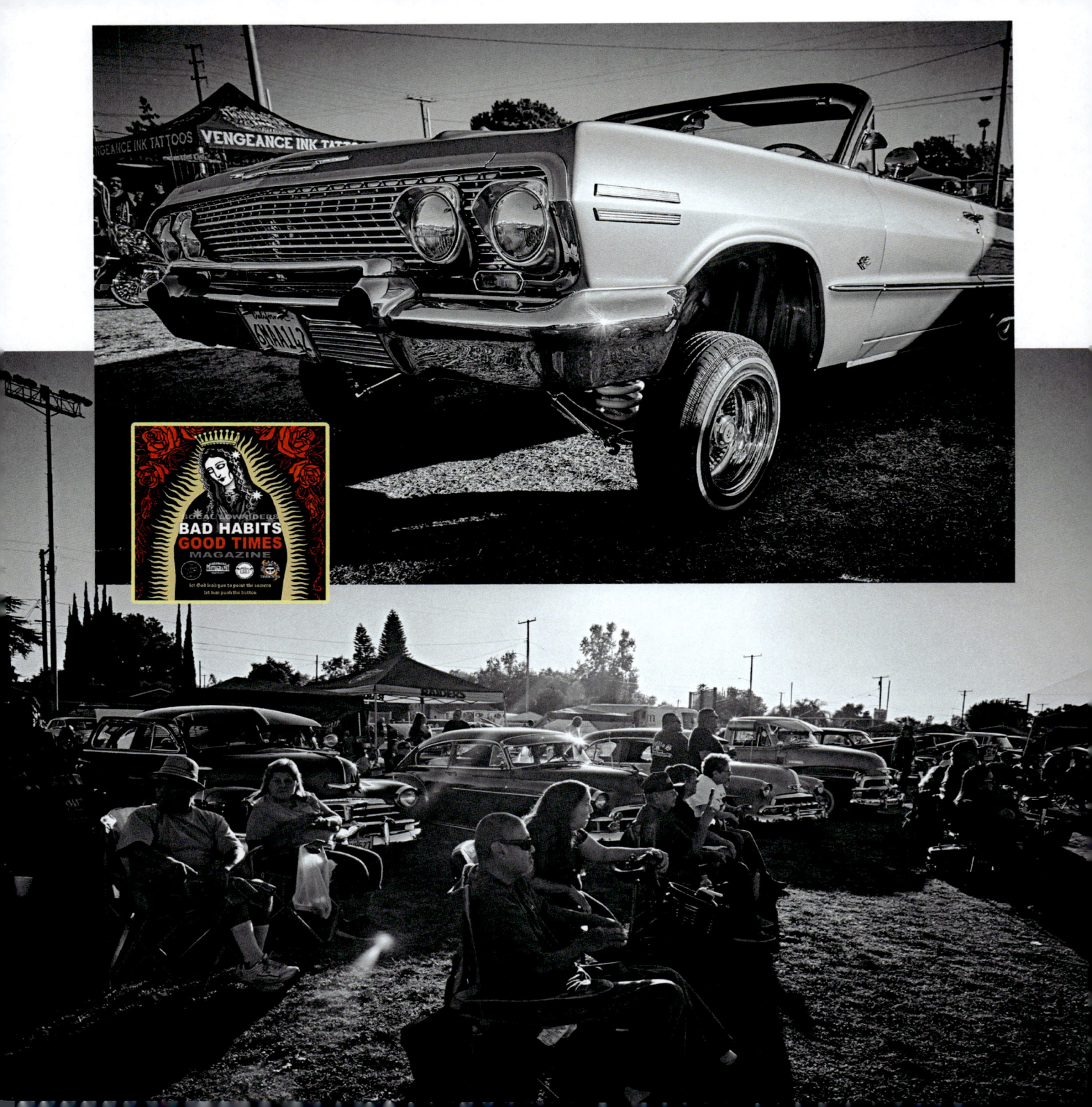

SOCAL LOWRIDERS
BAD HABITS
GOOD TIMES
MAGAZINE

let God lead you to point the camera
let him push the button

SOCAL LOWRIDERS
BAD HABITS
GOOD TIMES
DECEMBER 2024   VOLUME 22

BAD HABITS
GOOD TIMES

Elvia Cadena

**BAD HABITS
GOOD TIMES**

Unique Photography
High Desert

UNIQUE PHOTOGRAPHY
High Desert

UNIQUE
PHOTOGRAPHY
High Desert

BAD HABITS GOOD TIMES Services

engagement photography

ANGEL BABY OLDIES
DEDICATIONS & SHOUT OUTS

1. To the L.A. Dodgers from George Z
Ded: we are the Champions by Queen

2. To Christian Garcia From Frank Hats
Ded: I'm so Proud by the Impressions

4. The hid daughter Sabrina From Dad Pastor Shady
Ded: can't loose by following God by whole truth

5. To Carol from Mark in Ont
Just want let you know I am serious you are the one
Ded: The Bells by the Originals

6. To her Daughters from Leslie Altamirano
Ded: Pretty girl by MC Magic

7. To Tony Fr Bonnie
Ded: two lovers by Mary Wells

8. To Angie From Johnny Happy Happy Birthday!
Ded: Baby you got it by Brenton Wood

9. To Robert From Loca smiles
Ded: just be good to me by the S.O.S. band

3. Happy Birthday Tiny from Charlie Perez

10. To Dad Henry from the Chalupa Fam
Really Really miss you by Smokey Robinson

11. To Jessica From Lindsey
Ded: Flowers by the Emotions

12. To Danny From Marie
Ded: Love you so by Ron Holden

13. To all the Veterans from Angel Baby
Ded: a Prayer for my Soldier by Helen Curry "thank you for your service"

FOLLOW ME ON IG
@MR ANGEL BABY

SOCAL LOWRIDERS
BAD HABITS GOOD TIMES
BY JOSEPH CHAVEZ   VOLUME 15

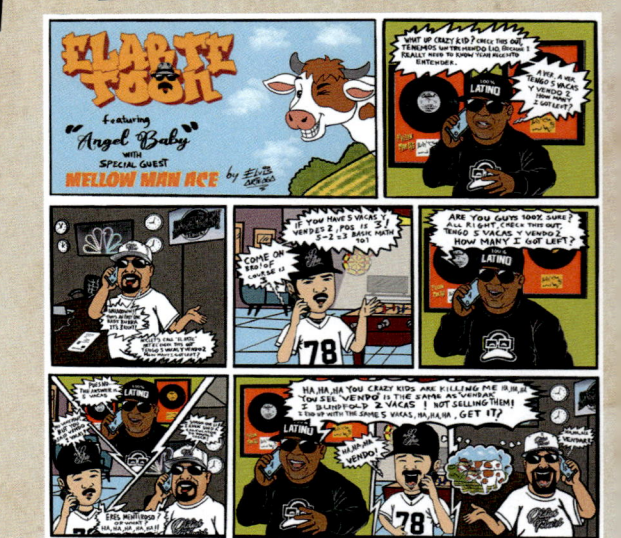

New toon drop each Friday Follow @ElArte78
& Mr_Angel_Baby on IG

OLDIES FOREVER

Dedications taken from Angel Baby LIVE Radio Show Fridays 6-9pm

**BAD HABITS
GOOD TIMES**

**CHRISTIAN
GARCIA**

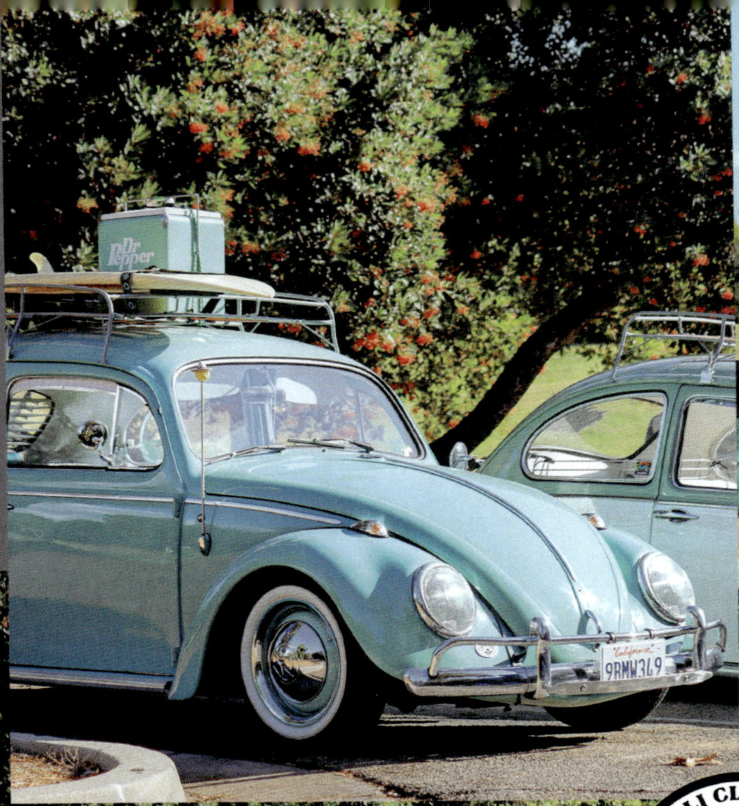

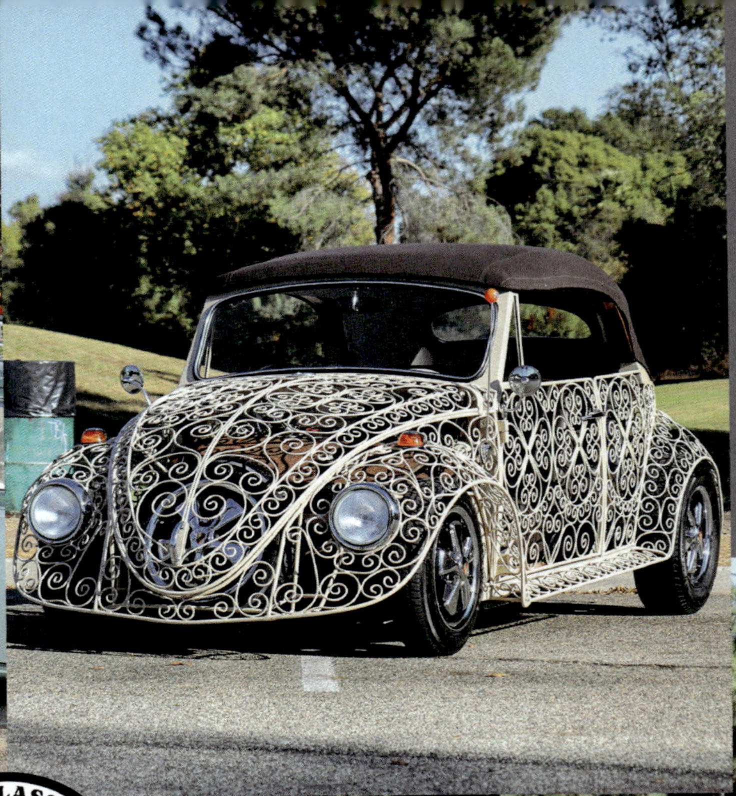

CALI CLASSICS
CHINO CALIFORNIA

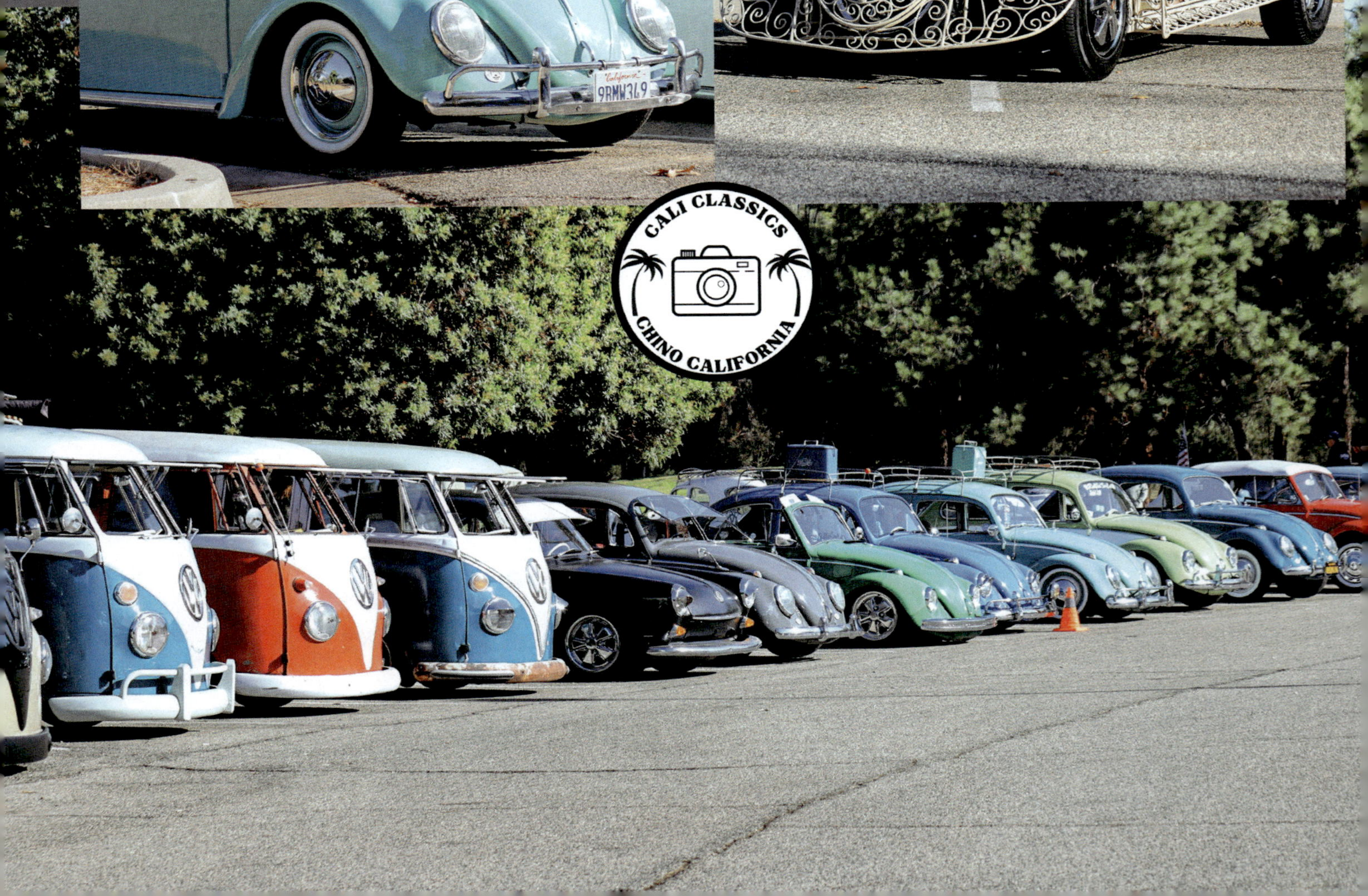

CALI CLASSICS CHINO CALIFORNIA

CALI CLASSICS
CHINO CALIFORNIA

CALIFORNIA 56
8MBU780

SOCAL LOWRIDERS
BAD HABITS
GOOD TIMES

December 2024 — VOLUME 24

**BAD HABITS
GOOD TIMES**

Dos Chicanos Podcast

OLDIES FOREVER

HTTP://FranksHatsGarciaHats.com

ANGELBABY OLDIES

BAD HABITS GOOD TIMES

SOCAL LOWRIDERS
BAD HABITS
GOOD TIMES
MAGAZINE

BAD HABITS
GOOD TIMES

PHOTO EXTRAS

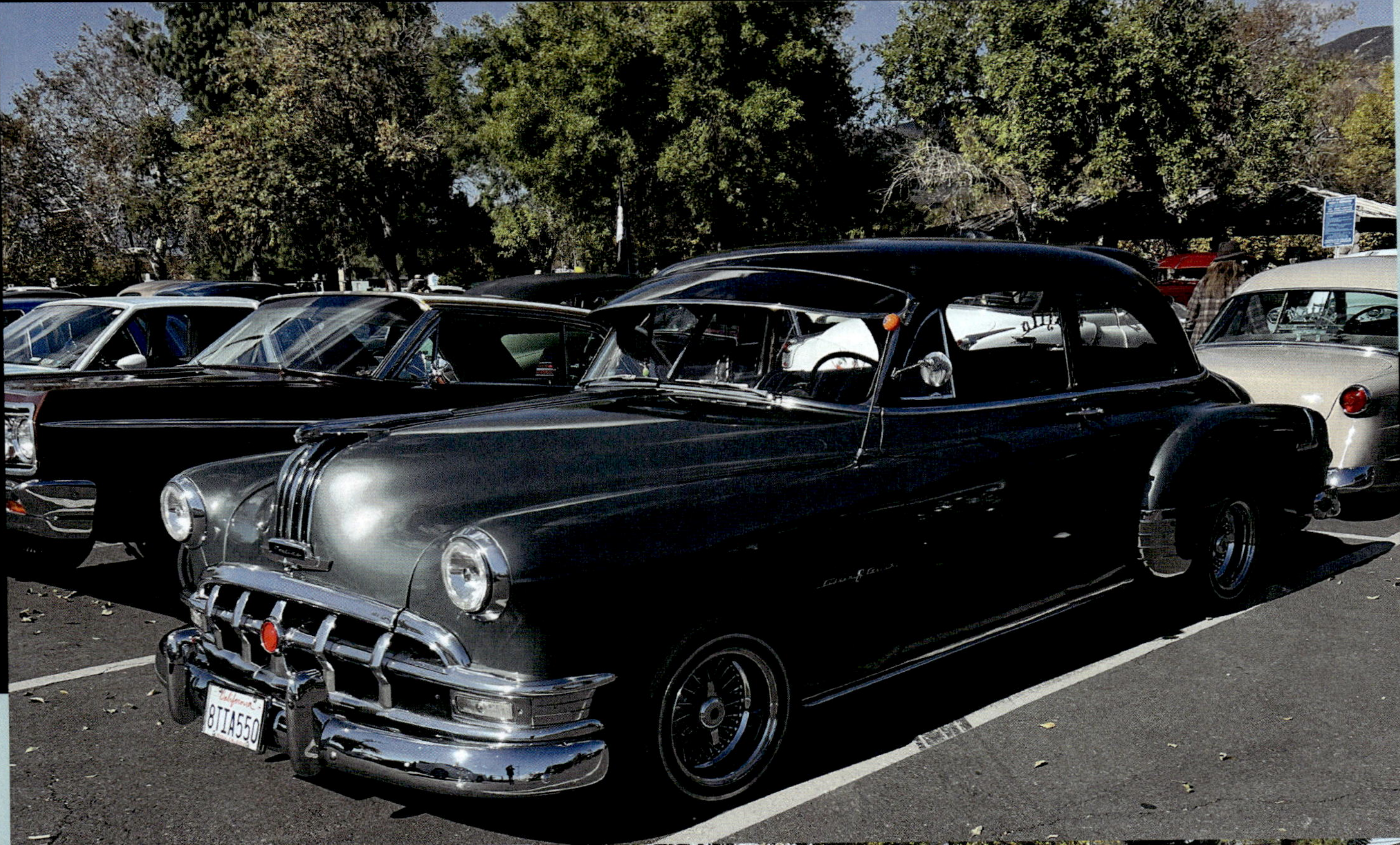

INLAND EMPIRE
CRUISE NITES

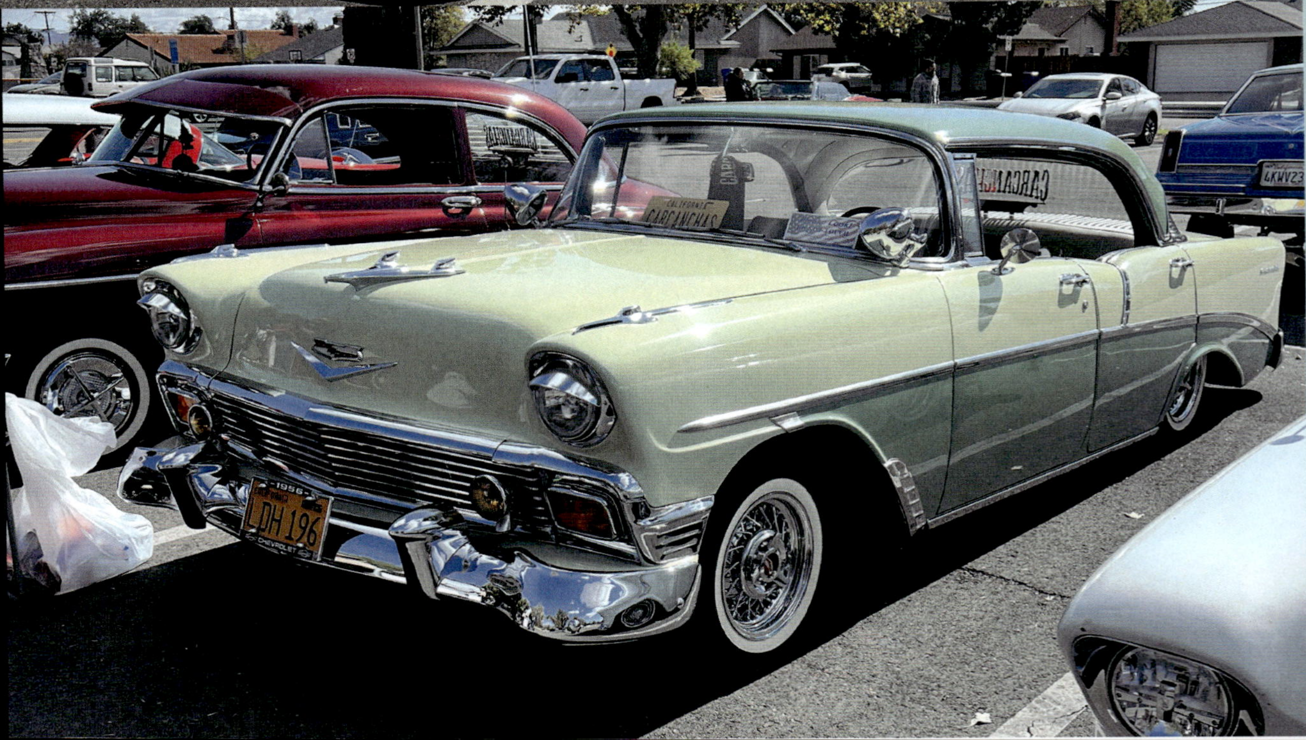

INLAND EMPIRE CRUISE NITES

Made in the USA
Las Vegas, NV
25 February 2025

18678052R00017